HUA HIN

2024

"Your Companion to witnessing the best of HUA HIN, day trip holiday, beaches, adventure, valentine's delight , culture and festival, top tourist attractions and hidden gems"

ANGELA DARLINGTON

1

TABLE OF CONTENTS

Introduction

About Hua Hin

Nestled in the Gulf of Thailand, Hua Hin is a charming coastal town renowned for its pristine beaches, rich cultural heritage, and a perfect blend of modern amenities with a touch of royal elegance. Originating as a quiet fishing village, Hua Hin has become a preferred destination for local and international travelers seeking a serene yet vibrant escape. The town, located approximately 200 kilometers south of Bangkok, boasts a unique charm that sets it apart from other popular Thai destinations.

Hua Hin's allure lies not only in its sun-kissed shores but also in its historical significance. Once a favored summer retreat for Thai royalty, particularly King Rama VII, Hua Hin preserves its regal ambiance, which is evident in the well-preserved palaces and royal residences dotting the landscape. Visitors are treated to a rare blend of traditional Thai hospitality and a laid-back beach atmosphere, making Hua Hin an ideal destination for those seeking a relaxing getaway without compromising cultural experiences.

Purpose of the Guide

The purpose of this travel guide is to serve as your comprehensive companion to Hua Hin, offering insights and recommendations to ensure an unforgettable journey. Whether you're a first-time visitor or a seasoned traveler, this guide aims to provide valuable information on planning your trip, navigating the local culture, and discovering the hidden gems that make Hua Hin a gem on the Thai coast.

We understand that each traveler is unique and seeks different experiences. This guide has been crafted to cater to a diverse range of interests. From historical landmarks to outdoor adventures, delectable cuisine, to vibrant markets, Hua Hin has something for everyone. We aim to empower you with the knowledge to tailor your visit to match your preferences and create memories that last a lifetime.

What's New in 2024

As of 2024, Hua Hin continues to evolve, embracing modernity while preserving its timeless appeal. Several exciting developments make this year an opportune time to explore the town:

1. Sustainable Tourism Initiatives

Hua Hin has taken significant strides in promoting sustainable tourism practices. Various eco-friendly initiatives have been implemented, from waste reduction programs to promoting responsible wildlife tourism. Travelers are encouraged to engage in environmentally conscious activities and support businesses that preserve the town's natural beauty.

2. Emerging Culinary Scene

While Hua Hin has long been celebrated for its traditional Thai cuisine, 2024 sees a vibrant and diverse culinary scene emerge. The town now boasts an array of international restaurants, fusion eateries, and trendy cafes, providing visitors with an expanded gastronomic palette.

3. Technology Integration for Convenience

Hua Hin embraces technology to enhance the visitor experience. Technology has been seamlessly integrated to make your stay more convenient and enjoyable, from user-friendly travel apps offering real-time information on local attractions to contactless payment options in hotels and restaurants.

4. Cultural Events and Festivals

In 2024, Hua Hin will host various cultural events and festivals that showcase the town's artistic spirit. From traditional music and dance performances to contemporary art exhibitions, these events provide a deeper understanding of Hua Hin's cultural tapestry and offer unique opportunities for cultural immersion.

5. Upgraded Accommodations

Several renowned hotels and resorts in Hua Hin have undergone renovations and expansions, offering upgraded facilities and services to cater to the evolving needs of travelers. Whether you seek a luxurious beachfront retreat or a cozy boutique stay, Hua Hin offers an even more diverse range of accommodations.

In conclusion, Hua Hin is a destination that seamlessly marries tradition with progress, offering a captivating experience for every traveler. This guide is your key to unlocking the secrets of Hua Hin, ensuring that your journey is well-informed and tailored to your preferences. Embrace the enchantment of Hua Hin in 2024 and embark on a voyage that promises relaxation and exploration.

Planning Your Trip

Best Time to Visit

Choosing the right time to visit Hua Hin ensures an optimal experience. The town enjoys a tropical climate, and the best time to visit largely depends on your preferences and the activities you have in mind. The high tourist season from November to February offers cool and dry weather, making it ideal for beach activities and outdoor exploration. However, this period tends to be busier, so early planning and reservations are advisable.

Suppose you prefer a more serene atmosphere and are willing to embrace a bit of rainfall. In that case, the shoulder seasons of March to May and June to October might be appealing. During these periods, Hua Hin experiences occasional rain showers. Still, the landscapes bloom in lush greenery, and the accommodations often offer lower rates.

How to Get There

By Air:

The most convenient way to reach Hua Hin is by flying into Bangkok's Suvarnabhumi Airport, an international hub with excellent connectivity. From the airport, you have several transportation options to Hua Hin:

- **Private Transfer:** Arrange for a private car transfer for a comfortable and direct journey to Hua Hin. Many hotels also provide airport transfer services.

- **Public Bus:** Economical and straightforward, buses regularly operate from the airport to Hua Hin. The journey takes approximately 3-4 hours, allowing you to enjoy the scenic landscapes.

By Train:

For a unique travel experience, consider taking the train from Bangkok to Hua Hin. The train journey offers stunning views of the Thai countryside, and the Hua Hin Railway Station, with its charming architecture, adds a touch of nostalgia to your arrival.

By Car:

If you enjoy the flexibility of driving, renting a car allows you to explore the surrounding areas at your own pace. The journey from Bangkok to Hua Hin takes approximately 2-3 hours, depending on traffic conditions.

Visa Information

As of 2024, many visitors to Hua Hin can enter Thailand visa-free for short stays. However, it's crucial to check the most recent visa regulations, as they can be subject to change. Travelers from certain countries may be eligible for a visa on arrival. In contrast, others might need to obtain one in advance.

Ensure that your passport is valid for at least six months beyond your intended departure date and that you comply with all visa requirements. Thai immigration authorities are generally accommodating, but having all the necessary documents is advisable to facilitate a smooth entry.

Currency and Money Matters

The official currency in Hua Hin, as in the rest of Thailand, is the Thai Baht (THB). While credit cards are widely accepted in hotels, restaurants, and larger establishments, carrying some cash for transactions in smaller shops, markets, and local eateries is advisable.

Currency exchange services are readily available in Hua Hin, particularly in the town center and major tourist areas. ATMs are also plentiful, providing convenient access to cash. Remember that some smaller establishments may only accept cash, so having a mix of payment options ensures a seamless shopping and dining experience.

Language and Communication

The primary language spoken in Hua Hin is Thai. While English is widely understood in tourist areas, learning a few basic Thai phrases is beneficial to enhance your interactions with locals. Thais appreciate visitors making an effort to speak their language, no matter how basic, which can lead to more enriching cultural experiences.

In Hua Hin, you'll find that many signage and information are also available in English. If you encounter language barriers, don't hesitate to use translation apps or seek assistance from your accommodation's concierge. Thais are known for their hospitality and are often more than willing to help visitors navigate the town.

In conclusion, meticulous planning is key to a successful trip to Hua Hin. From selecting the optimal time to visit to understanding visa requirements and familiarizing yourself with local currency and language, these considerations contribute to a seamless and enjoyable travel experience. As you embark on your journey to Hua Hin, embrace the excitement of exploration and the warmth of Thai hospitality.

Accommodation

Choosing the right accommodation is pivotal to crafting a memorable experience when planning your visit to Hua Hin. Whether you're seeking luxury, budget-friendly options or unique stays that offer a distinct flavor of Hua Hin, the town caters to diverse preferences. This section will guide you through the various accommodation options and provide essential booking tips to ensure a comfortable and enjoyable stay.

Top Hotels and Resorts

Hua Hin boasts an array of luxurious hotels and resorts that combine world-class amenities with breathtaking views and impeccable service. Here are some of the top establishments that redefine the meaning of hospitality in Hua Hin:

a. Centara Grand Beach Resort & Villas Hua Hin:

- Nestled on the beachfront, this iconic resort exudes colonial charm. Centara Grand Beach Resort & Villas Hua Hin is a haven for those seeking a sophisticated retreat with its lush gardens, multiple dining options, and a spa offering rejuvenating treatments.

b. Anantara Hua Hin Resort:

- Set amidst 14 acres of tropical gardens, Anantara Hua Hin Resort offers a blend of Thai architecture and modern luxury. Guests can enjoy the beachfront pool and spa treatments and savor culinary delights at on-site restaurants.

c. Chiva-Som International Health Resort:

- Renowned as one of the world's premier wellness retreats, Chiva-Som focuses on holistic health and relaxation. This resort provides an exclusive and rejuvenating experience, from tailored spa programs to exquisite dining.

Budget-Friendly Options

For travelers seeking comfortable yet affordable accommodations, Hua Hin offers a range of budget-friendly options that don't compromise on quality or convenience:

a. Ibis Hua Hin Hotel:

- Situated in the heart of Hua Hin, Ibis Hua Hin Hotel provides modern and cozy rooms at an affordable price. With its central Location, guests can easily access the town's attractions, markets, and vibrant nightlife.

b. My Way Hua Hin Music Hotel:

- This unique and budget-friendly hotel combines the love of music with comfortable lodging. Each room is themed around a different music genre, providing a quirky and memorable stay for music enthusiasts on a budget.

c. Baan Taweesuk Guesthouse:

- A charming guesthouse near the night market, Baan Taweesuk offers clean and cozy rooms with a homely atmosphere. It's an excellent choice for budget-conscious travelers looking for a centrally located stay.

Unique Stays in Hua Hin

For those seeking an extraordinary and culturally immersive experience, Hua Hin provides unique accommodation options that go beyond the ordinary:

a. Aka Resort Hua Hin:

- Tucked away in lush surroundings, Aka Resort offers private pool villas with a distinct design inspired by traditional Thai architecture. It provides an intimate and serene escape from the hustle and bustle of the town.

b. Let's Sea Hua Hin Al Fresco Resort:

- This beachfront resort takes the concept of open-air living to a new level. With rooms that feature private terraces with direct access to the pool, Let's Sea Hua Hin Al Fresco Resort offers a refreshing and innovative approach to luxury accommodation.

c. Baba Beach Club Hua Hin Luxury Pool Villa Hotel by Sri Panwa:

- Blending contemporary design with a vibrant atmosphere, this luxury pool villa hotel is renowned for its stylish accommodations and beachfront Location. Each villa is a private oasis, complete with a personal infinity pool.

Booking Tips

When booking accommodations in Hua Hin, consider the following tips to make the most of your stay:

a. Book in Advance:

- Especially during the high season, booking your accommodation well in advance is advisable to secure your preferred choice and benefit from early booking discounts.

b. Read Reviews:

- Utilize online platforms to read reviews from fellow travelers. Real experiences can provide valuable insights into the quality of service, amenities, and overall guest satisfaction.

c. Check for Deals and Packages:

- Many hotels in Hua Hin offer special deals and packages that may include complimentary meals, spa treatments, or discounts on local attractions. Keep an eye out for these promotions to enhance your overall experience.

d. Consider Location:

- Choose accommodation based on your planned activities. If you seek a beach retreat, opt for beachfront resorts. For easy access to markets and nightlife, stay in the town center.

e. Contact the Hotel Directly:

- Before booking, consider reaching out to the hotel directly. This can sometimes result in special arrangements, room upgrades, or personalized services that enhance your stay.

In conclusion, Hua Hin's accommodations cater to diverse preferences and budgets, ensuring every traveler finds a home away from home. Whether you're indulging in luxury, seeking affordability, or craving a unique stay, Hua Hin's lodging options contribute to the overall charm of this coastal town.

Exploring Hua Hin

Hua Hin Attractions

1. Hua Hin Beach:

Hua Hin's main attraction is its pristine beach stretching along the Gulf of Thailand. The long, sandy shoreline is perfect for strolls, water sports, or basking in the sun. The beach is lined with vibrant restaurants, bars, and shops, creating a lively atmosphere against the backdrop of the azure sea.

2. Cicada Market:

Cicada Market is a vibrant night market that showcases the local arts scene. Open only on weekends, it's a treasure trove of handmade crafts, artwork, and unique souvenirs. Live performances, cultural displays, and various delectable street foods make Cicada Market a must-visit for those wanting to immerse themselves in Hua Hin's creative spirit.

Historical Sites

1. Phra Ratchaniwet Marukhathaiyawan (Mrigadayavan Palace):

Built during the reign of King Rama VI, this teakwood palace served as the summer residence for the Thai royal family. The architectural beauty, surrounded by lush gardens and overlooking the sea, provides a glimpse into Thailand's regal past. Visitors can explore the well-preserved halls and chambers, each with a unique charm.

2. Hua Hin Railway Station:

Dating back to the early 20th century, the Hua Hin Railway Station is a transportation hub and an architectural gem. The station's royal waiting room, constructed in a Thai royal pavilion style, showcases intricate woodwork and is a testament to the town's historical significance as a royal retreat.

Natural Wonders

1. Khao Takiab (Monkey Mountain):

For a dose of nature and wildlife, venture to Khao Takiab, also known as Monkey Mountain. The hill is home to a Buddhist temple and offers panoramic views of Hua Hin. Visitors can interact with the resident monkeys, explore the temple grounds, and enjoy a hike to the summit for breathtaking vistas.

2. Sam Roi Yot National Park:

A short drive from Hua Hin, Sam Roi Yot National Park is a haven for nature lovers. The park is known for its limestone hills, caves, and diverse ecosystems. The highlight is Phraya Nakhon Cave, featuring a stunning pavilion bathed in natural light. This sight has made it one of Thailand's most photographed locations.

Entertainment and Nightlife

1. Hua Hin Night Market:

As the sun sets, Hua Hin's Night Market comes to life. Stretching along the town's main road, the market offers a lively atmosphere with street performers, traditional Thai music, and an array of stalls selling everything from local delicacies to clothing and handicrafts. It's an excellent place to experience the local culture and sample authentic Thai street food.

2. Jazz Music at Hua Hin Hills Vineyard:

For a more refined evening, head to Hua Hin Hills Vineyard. The venue hosts jazz performances against the backdrop of vineyards, creating a relaxing and sophisticated ambiance. Visitors can savor local wines, enjoy a gourmet meal, and unwind with live music in this unique setting.

Day Trips and Excursions

1. Pranburi Forest Park:

Approximately 30 minutes south of Hua Hin, Pranburi Forest Park offers a serene escape into nature. The park features wooden boardwalks through mangrove forests, providing an opportunity to spot various bird species and other wildlife. The peaceful surroundings make it an ideal day trip for nature enthusiasts.

2. Pala-U Waterfall:

Nature lovers and adventure seekers will appreciate a day trip to Pala-U Waterfall. Located within Kaeng Krachan National Park, this multi-tiered waterfall is surrounded by lush greenery and offers a refreshing escape. Visitors can trek through the park, swim in natural pools, and relish the tranquility of the tropical rainforest.

Local Events and Festivals

1. Hua Hin Jazz Festival:

Held annually, the Hua Hin Jazz Festival attracts music enthusiasts worldwide. The event features performances by local and international jazz artists against the backdrop of the beach, creating a magical fusion of music and seaside ambiance.

2. Songkran (Thai New Year) Celebrations:

Songkran, the Thai New Year, is celebrated with fervor in Hua Hin. Usually occurring in April, the town comes alive with water fights, traditional ceremonies, and cultural events. Joining in the water festivities is a unique way to experience the joy and warmth of Thai hospitality.

In conclusion, exploring Hua Hin offers diverse experiences, from historical and cultural immersion to natural wonders and vibrant nightlife. Whether lounging on the beach, delving into the town's rich history, or venturing on day trips to nearby attractions, Hua Hin ensures that every traveler finds something to capture their heart and create lasting memories.

Dining and Cuisine

Local Thai Delicacies

1. Som Tum (Green Papaya Salad):

A quintessential Thai dish, Som Tum is a refreshing salad made with shredded green papaya, cherry tomatoes, beans, peanuts, and chilies. Combining sweet, sour, and spicy flavors creates a delightful culinary experience. Som Tum is perfect for those seeking a light and flavorful appetizer.

2. Tom Yum Goong (Spicy Shrimp Soup):

Tom Yum Goong is a hot and sour soup featuring succulent shrimp, fragrant herbs, lemongrass, and chili. The rich broth, infused with the vibrant flavors of Thai spices, is a beloved comfort food embodying Thai cuisine's essence. It's often enjoyed with a side of steamed rice.

3. Pad Thai:

All exploration of Thai cuisine is complete with savoring Pad Thai. This iconic stir-fried noodle dish combines rice noodles, tofu or shrimp, bean sprouts, peanuts, and lime. The balance of sweet, salty, and tangy flavors makes Pad Thai a universally loved dish showcasing Thai culinary traditions' artistry.

International Cuisine

Hua Hin's culinary landscape extends beyond traditional Thai fare, offering diverse international cuisines to cater to its multicultural visitors.

1. La Terrasse:

For a taste of authentic French cuisine, La Terrasse is a charming restaurant set in a colonial-style house. This establishment provides a delightful fusion of French elegance and Thai hospitality with a menu featuring classic French dishes such as Coq au Vin and Beef Bourguignon.

2. Big Fish Seafood Restaurant:

Seafood enthusiasts will appreciate the offerings at Big Fish Seafood Restaurant. Overlooking the Gulf of Thailand, this establishment specializes in fresh seafood with a Thai twist. From grilled prawns to seafood curry, the menu showcases the sea's bounty in a picturesque setting.

Popular Restaurants and Street Food

1. Chote Chitr:

For an authentic Thai dining experience, Chote Chitr is a hidden gem. Tucked away in the old quarter of Hua Hin, this restaurant serves traditional Thai dishes, focusing on bold and flavorful curries. The intimate setting and attentive service add to the overall charm of the dining experience.

2. Hua Hin Night Market Street Food:

Hua Hin's Night Market is a culinary paradise for street food enthusiasts. As the sun sets, the market comes alive with various stalls offering grilled meats, seafood, noodles, and delectable desserts. Try the famous Hua Hin-style fried mussels or explore the diverse flavors of Thai street food as you stroll through the bustling market.

Dining Etiquette

While enjoying the diverse culinary offerings in Hua Hin, it's essential to be mindful of Thai dining etiquette to appreciate the cultural nuances associated with the dining experience fully.

1. Traditional Greetings:

Upon entering a restaurant, it's customary to offer a polite greeting known as the "wai." This involves placing your palms together in a prayer-like gesture and bowing slightly. The higher the hands, the more respect is conveyed.

2. Sharing is Caring:

Thai meals are often communal, with dishes placed in the center of the table for everyone to share. Taking small portions is customary to avoid wasting food, and sharing fosters a sense of community and friendliness.

3. Chopsticks and Spoons:

While chopsticks are commonly used for noodle dishes, Thai meals typically involve a spoon and fork. The fork is used to push food onto the spoon, which is then brought to the mouth. Chopsticks are reserved for specific dishes, and asking for a fork is acceptable if you're more comfortable with one.

4. Show Respect to Elders:

In Thai culture, showing respect to elders is of utmost importance. When dining with older individuals, wait for them to eat before you start.

This demonstrates reverence and is considered polite.

5. Tipping Etiquette:

Tipping is not mandatory in Thailand, but it is appreciated. A customary tip is around 10% of the bill. In some upscale restaurants, a service charge may be included, so checking before tipping is advisable.

In conclusion, dining in Hua Hin is a culinary journey that encapsulates the rich flavors of Thai cuisine alongside a diverse range of international offerings. From local delicacies that tantalize the taste buds to the international gourmet scene and the vibrant street food culture, Hua Hin's dining landscape reflects its cultural diversity and welcoming hospitality. Embrace the local dining etiquette to enhance your gastronomic experience and create lasting memories of your culinary adventures in this coastal gem.

Outdoor Activities

Beach Activities

1. Relaxation and Sunbathing:

Hua Hin's expansive beaches, with their golden sands and gentle waves, provide the perfect setting for relaxation and sunbathing. Whether you unwind with a good book, stroll along the shore, or bask in the sun, Hua Hin's beaches offer a serene escape from the hustle and bustle of everyday life.

2. Horseback Riding:

For a unique beach experience, consider horseback riding along the shore. Several operators offer horse riding services, allowing you to explore the coastline on horseback. It's a picturesque way to appreciate the beauty of Hua Hin's beaches while enjoying freedom and tranquility.

Water Sports

1. Kitesurfing:

With its consistent winds and expansive coastline, Hua Hin has become a popular destination for kitesurfing enthusiasts. Whether you're a seasoned pro or a beginner, numerous schools along the beach offer lessons and equipment rental. Glide across the waves and feel the adrenaline rush as you harness the power of the wind.

2. Jet Skiing and Parasailing:

Adventurous visitors can enjoy thrilling water sports such as jet skiing and parasailing. Rental services are available on the main beaches, providing an opportunity to experience the excitement of speeding across the water or soaring through the sky while enjoying panoramic views of the coastline.

Golf Courses

1. Black Mountain Golf Club:

Hua Hin has earned a reputation as a premier destination for golf enthusiasts, and the Black Mountain Golf Club stands as a testament to the town's golfing prowess. This award-winning golf course offers a challenging yet scenic experience, with lush green fairways surrounded by the natural beauty of the Thai landscape.

2. Banyan Golf Club:

Another gem in Hua Hin's golfing crown is the Banyan Golf Club. Renowned for its impeccable course design and stunning views of the surrounding hills, this club provides an enjoyable and challenging golfing experience. After a round of golf, relax at the club's facilities, including a spa and restaurant.

Hiking and Nature Trails

1. Khao Sam Roi Yot National Park:

Nature enthusiasts and hikers will find Khao Sam Roi Yot National Park a haven of biodiversity and scenic beauty. The park, a short drive from Hua Hin, features limestone hills, caves, and diverse ecosystems. Trails lead to viewpoints overlooking the Gulf of Thailand and offer opportunities to spot wildlife amid the lush surroundings.

2. Hin Lek Fai Viewpoint:

For a panoramic view of Hua Hin and its surroundings, trek to the Hin Lek Fai Viewpoint. While relatively easy, the hike rewards adventurers with breathtaking vistas of the town, the coastline, and the distant hills. It's an ideal spot to witness the sunset and capture stunning photographs.

In conclusion, Hua Hin's outdoor activities cater to a spectrum of interests, from those seeking relaxation on the beach to adrenaline junkies eager to conquer the waves. Golf enthusiasts can hone their skills on world-class courses. At the same time, nature lovers can explore the scenic beauty of national parks and hiking trails. Whatever your preference, Hua Hin's outdoor offerings ensure a well-rounded and enjoyable experience amidst the natural splendor of this coastal gem. Whether you're teeing off on a lush golf course, feeling the wind in your hair during water sports, or immersing yourself in the tranquility of nature trails, Hua Hin invites you to embrace the great outdoors in diverse and exciting ways.

Shopping

Popular Shopping Districts

1. Cicada Market:

Cicada Market is not just a haven for art enthusiasts; it's also a vibrant shopping district. This weekend market showcases many handmade crafts, unique artwork, clothing, and accessories. It's a perfect place to discover one-of-a-kind items created by local artists. The market's lively atmosphere, with live performances and cultural displays, adds to the shopping experience.

2. Hua Hin Night Market:

Hua Hin Night Market is an iconic shopping destination that comes alive as the sun sets. Stretching along the town's main road, this bustling market offers diverse products, from clothing and accessories to souvenirs and street food. It's a fantastic place to immerse yourself in the local culture, haggle for bargains, and sample delicious Thai street food.

Traditional Markets

1. Chatchai Market:

For an authentic Thai market experience, Chatchai Market is a bustling local market where residents shop for fresh produce, seafood, and household goods. The market provides a glimpse into the daily lives of locals, and visitors can explore stalls selling everything from tropical fruits to aromatic spices. It's an excellent place to experience the vibrant energy of Hua Hin's local market scene.

2. Sam Phan Nam Floating Market:

Sam Phan Nam Floating Market adds a unique twist to traditional market shopping. Set within a village-inspired layout, this market features wooden walkways along the water, creating a charming atmosphere. Visitors can shop for local products, enjoy boat rides, and savor authentic Thai snacks while enjoying the picturesque surroundings.

Boutique Stores and Malls

1. Hua Hin Market Village:

Hua Hin Market Village is a modern shopping complex that caters to various tastes. This mall offers a diverse shopping experience, from international brands to local boutiques. Visitors can explore fashion outlets and electronics stores and dine in various restaurants. The mall's convenient Location in the town center makes it a popular choice for those seeking a mix of local and international shopping options.

2. Bluport Hua Hin Resort Mall:

Bluport Hua Hin Resort Mall is a stylish and contemporary shopping destination. With a focus on high-end fashion, lifestyle products, and dining, this mall caters to those looking for a sophisticated shopping experience. The mall's architecture and design create a relaxed and upscale atmosphere, making it a favored choice for discerning shoppers.

Souvenirs and Local Crafts

1. Plearnwan Vintage Village:

Plearnwan Vintage Village is not just a shopping destination; it's a step back in time. This retro-themed village features shops selling vintage-style souvenirs, clothing, and accessories. Visitors can explore the quaint streets, take a trip down memory lane, and shop for unique items that capture the charm of yesteryears.

2. Hua Hin Handicraft Center:

The Hua Hin Handicraft Center is a treasure trove for those interested in authentic local crafts. This center showcases a variety of handmade products crafted by local artisans, including traditional Thai textiles, ceramics, and woodwork. It's an ideal place to find meaningful souvenirs that reflect the cultural heritage of Hua Hin.

Shopping Tips for Hua Hin

1. **Bargaining:** Bargaining is a common practice in markets and smaller shops. Polite negotiation can lead to favorable deals, but it's important to do so with respect and a friendly demeanor.

2. **Cash is King:** While credit cards are widely accepted in malls and larger establishments, having cash on hand is advisable when shopping in traditional markets or smaller shops.

3. **Check Opening Hours:** Cicada Market and Hua Hin Night Market operate during specific hours, usually in the evenings. Confirm the opening hours to plan your shopping excursions accordingly.

4. **Explore Off the Beaten Path:** Venture beyond the main shopping areas to discover hidden gems. Local neighborhoods often have small shops and markets with unique products and a more authentic atmosphere.

5. **Support Local Artisans:** Consider purchasing products directly from local artisans at markets like Cicada Market. This ensures the authenticity of the items and supports the livelihoods of talented individuals in the community.

In conclusion, shopping in Hua Hin is a delightful adventure offering diverse experiences, from exploring traditional markets to indulging in upscale boutiques. Whether you're seeking unique handmade crafts, trendy fashion, or vintage treasures, Hua Hin's shopping scene has something for everyone. Embrace the local culture, haggle for bargains, and return from your trip with memories and a bag full of souvenirs that reflect the vibrant spirit of this coastal town.

Sample Itinerary

Day 1: Arrival and Beachfront Bliss

Morning:

- **Arrival at Hua Hin:**
  - Start your journey by arriving in Hua Hin by car or train from Bangkok.
  - Check into your chosen accommodation and freshen up for the exciting days ahead.

Afternoon:

- **Lunch at Chote Chitr:**
  - Head to Chote Chitr, a hidden gem serving authentic Thai cuisine. Savor traditional dishes in a charming setting.

- **Explore Hua Hin Beach:**
  - After lunch, take a stroll along the iconic Hua Hin Beach.
  - Engage in beach activities or relax on the sandy shores.

Evening:

- **Dinner at Hua Hin Night Market:**

    - Dive into the vibrant atmosphere of Hua Hin Night Market.

    - Sample local street food, shop for souvenirs, and soak in the lively ambiance.

Day 2: Cultural Immersion and Nature Retreat

Morning:

- **Breakfast at a Local Café:**

    - Start your day with a delicious breakfast at one of Hua Hin's quaint local cafes.

- **Visit Mrigadayavan Palace:**

    - Explore the historical Mrigadayavan Palace, once the royal summer residence.

    - Marvel at the exquisite teakwood architecture and lush surroundings.

Afternoon:

- **Lunch at Let's Sea Hua Hin Al Fresco Resort:**

  - Enjoy a beachfront lunch at Let's Sea Hua Hin Al Fresco Resort, known for its innovative cuisine.

- **Hin Lek Fai Viewpoint Hike:**

  - Embark on a scenic hike to Hin Lek Fai Viewpoint for panoramic views of Hua Hin and the coastline.

Evening:

- **Dinner at Cicada Market:**

  - Head to Cicada Market for an art, music, and delectable street food evening.

  - Explore the vibrant stalls and enjoy live performances.

Day 3: Adventure and Waterfront Delights

Morning:

- **Breakfast at Ibis Hua Hin Hotel:**

  - Fuel up with breakfast at Ibis Hua Hin Hotel before your day of adventure.

- **Kitesurfing Adventure:**
  - Indulge your adventurous side with a kitesurfing lesson or session.
  - Experience the thrill of gliding over the waves.

Afternoon:

- **Lunch at Hua Hin Hills Vineyard:**
  - Head to Hua Hin Hills Vineyard for a unique lunch experience amid the vineyards.
  - Enjoy a gourmet meal and sample local wines.

- **Explore Sam Roi Yot National Park:**
  - Take an afternoon trip to Sam Roi Yot National Park.
  - Explore nature trails, visit Phraya Nakhon Cave, and soak in the natural beauty.

Evening:

- **Seafood Dinner at Big Fish Seafood Restaurant:**
  - Indulge in a seafood feast with a seaside view at Big Fish Seafood Restaurant.
  - Try the catch of the day prepared with local flavors.

Day 4: Golfing Extravaganza and Shopping Spree

Morning:

- **Morning Tee Time at Black Mountain Golf Club:**
  - Tee off at Black Mountain Golf Club, one of Hua Hin's premier golf courses.
  - Enjoy a challenging round surrounded by picturesque landscapes.

Afternoon:

- **Lunch at Bluport Hua Hin Resort Mall:**
    - Head to Bluport Hua Hin Resort Mall for a leisurely lunch.
    - Explore the upscale mall's fashion and lifestyle offerings.
- **Shopping at Cicada Market:**
    - Return to Cicada Market for some daytime shopping.
    - Browse through unique arts and crafts stalls for souvenirs.

Evening:

- **Dinner at Plearnwan Vintage Village:**
    - Experience the charm of Plearnwan Vintage Village for dinner.
    - Enjoy a meal in a retro-themed setting with a nostalgic ambiance.

Day 5: Relaxation and Departure

Morning:

- **Morning at Aka Resort Hua Hin:**

  - If time allows, spend a relaxing morning at Aka Resort Hua Hin.

  - Enjoy the private pool villas and serene surroundings.

Afternoon:

- **Lunch and Farewell at Baan Taweesuk Guesthouse:**

  - Have a farewell lunch at Baan Taweesuk Guesthouse, a charming local establishment.

- **Final Moments on Hua Hin Beach:**

  - Take a final stroll along Hua Hin Beach, capturing the essence of your trip.

  - Reflect on the memories created in this enchanting coastal town.

Evening:

- **Departure from Hua Hin:**
    - Check out of your accommodation and depart for your next destination or head back to Bangkok.

    - Bid farewell to Hua Hin with a heart full of memories.

This sample itinerary is a balanced blend of cultural exploration, outdoor adventures, culinary delights, and relaxation. Feel free to customize it based on your preferences and the duration of your stay. Whether you're an art lover, an adrenaline seeker, a nature enthusiast, or a golf fan, Hua Hin offers a diverse range of experiences to make your visit unforgettable.

Practical Tips

Transportation within Hua Hin

1. Tuk-Tuks and Taxis:

Hua Hin has a well-established network of tuk-tuks and taxis for convenient local transportation. Tuk-tuks are a fun and inexpensive way to navigate short distances. At the same time, taxis provide a comfortable option for longer journeys. Ensure that the fare is agreed upon before starting the ride.

2. Rental Scooters and Bicycles:

For a more adventurous exploration, consider renting a scooter or bicycle. Hua Hin's relatively flat terrain makes cycling enjoyable, and scooters allow one to explore nearby attractions independently. Rental services are widely available but always prioritize safety and wearing helmets when riding.

3. Songthaews (Shared Vans):

Songthaews, or shared vans, are a cost-effective means of getting around Hua Hin and neighboring areas. These shared vehicles follow specific routes and can be flagged down like buses. They offer an authentic local experience and are budget-friendly.

Health and Safety

1. Hydration and Sun Protection:

Given Hua Hin's tropical climate, staying hydrated and protecting yourself from the sun is crucial. Carry a water bottle, use sunscreen, and wear a hat or sunglasses to shield yourself from the sun's intense rays, especially during outdoor activities.

2. Mosquito Protection:

Thailand, like many tropical destinations, has mosquitoes. Use insect repellent, especially during the evening and in areas with dense vegetation. Wearing long sleeves and pants can provide additional protection, particularly in nature reserves or parks.

3. Local Healthcare Services:

Familiarize yourself with the Location of local healthcare facilities, such as hospitals and clinics. Hua Hin has reputable medical services, and it's wise to know where to seek assistance in case of any health concerns.

4. Travel Insurance:

Consider obtaining comprehensive travel insurance before your trip. This can cover medical emergencies, trip cancellations, and unexpected events, providing peace of mind during your stay.

Shopping Guide

1. Bargaining:

Bargaining is a common practice in Hua Hin's markets and smaller shops. Approach negotiations with a friendly attitude, and be prepared to haggle for better prices. It's part of the local shopping experience.

2. Local Currency:

While credit cards are widely accepted in malls and upscale establishments, smaller shops and markets may prefer cash. Ensure you have Thai Baht for transactions in traditional markets and local stores.

3. Opening Hours:

Be mindful of the opening hours of shops and markets, especially in smaller towns or during public holidays. Many markets, like Cicada Market and Hua Hin Night Market, are evening events. At the same time, some boutique stores may have varied schedules.

4. Authenticity of Souvenirs:

When purchasing souvenirs, especially handmade crafts, consider buying directly from local artisans or reputable markets like Cicada Market. This ensures the authenticity of the items and supports the local community.

Communication and Connectivity

1. Language:

English is widely spoken in tourist areas, but learning a few basic Thai phrases as a gesture of respect is helpful. Locals appreciate visitors making an effort to communicate in their language.

2. SIM Cards and Mobile Data:

Purchase a local SIM card upon arrival at the airport or in town to stay connected during your stay. Thailand has reliable mobile networks, and having a local number is useful for navigation and communication.

3. Internet Connectivity:

Many hotels, restaurants, and cafes offer free Wi-Fi. However, you plan to explore remote areas or natural parks. In that case, it's advisable to download maps or information in advance, as connectivity may be limited in certain regions.

4. Cultural Sensitivity:

Thailand is known for its rich cultural traditions. Show respect by dressing modestly, particularly when visiting temples or religious sites. Removing your shoes before entering someone's home or a sacred space is customary.

In conclusion, incorporating these practical tips into your Hua Hin adventure will create a smoother and more enjoyable experience. From navigating the town's diverse transportation options to staying healthy in the tropical climate, these guidelines aim to enhance every aspect of your visit. Embrace the local culture, savor the unique shopping experiences, and stay connected while immersing yourself in the beauty of Hua Hin.

Frequently Asked Questions (FAQs)

General Travel FAQs

Q: What is the local currency in Hua Hin?

A: The official currency of Thailand is the Thai Baht (THB). Currency exchange services are widely available in Hua Hin, and major credit cards are accepted in hotels, restaurants, and larger establishments. Carrying some cash is advisable, especially when shopping in local markets or smaller establishments.

Q: Is it safe to drink tap water?

A: While tap water in Hua Hin undergoes treatment, it is recommended to drink bottled or filtered water to avoid any potential stomach discomfort. Most hotels and restaurants provide complimentary bottled water, and it's widely available for purchase.

Planning FAQs

Q: How can I extend my visa if needed?

A: If you plan to extend your stay in Thailand, visit the Immigration Bureau in Hua Hin to inquire about visa extensions. It's essential to check the specific requirements and processing fees. Extensions may be granted for tourism, business, or other purposes.

Q: Are there any cultural norms I should be aware of?

A: Respecting Thai cultural norms is important. When visiting temples, dress modestly, covering shoulders and knees. Remove your shoes before entering someone's home or a sacred space. The traditional "wai" greeting involves placing your palms together and bowing slightly.

Accommodation FAQs

Q: What are the popular areas to stay in Hua Hin?

A: Hua Hin offers a range of accommodation options in various areas. Popular choices include:

- **Hua Hin Beach:** Ideal for beachfront resorts and proximity to the town's attractions.

- **Khao Takiab:** A quieter area with beachfront resorts and the famous Monkey Mountain.

- **Hua Hin City Center:** Convenient for shopping, dining, and exploring the town's cultural sites.

Q: How far in advance should I book my accommodation?

A: It's advisable to book accommodation in advance, especially during peak seasons or popular events. Booking early ensures a wider selection of options and better rates. However, spontaneous travelers can find last-minute deals, especially during the off-peak periods.

Dining and Cuisine FAQs

Q: Are vegetarian and vegan options readily available?

A: Yes, Hua Hin caters to various dietary preferences. Many restaurants offer vegetarian and vegan dishes, and you can find dedicated vegetarian eateries. Thai cuisine often includes plant-based options, and chefs usually accommodate dietary requirements.

Q: What are some must-try local dishes?

A: Hua Hin boasts a rich culinary scene, and some must-try local dishes include:

- **Som Tum (Green Papaya Salad):** A refreshing and spicy salad.

- **Tom Yum Goong (Spicy Shrimp Soup):** A flavorful and aromatic Thai soup.

- **Pad Thai:** Stir-fried noodles with a perfect blend of sweet, sour, and savory flavors.

- **Massaman Curry:** A fragrant and mildly spiced curry with influences from Persian cuisine.

- **Hua Hin-style Fried Mussels:** A local delicacy often found at night markets.

Whether you're a first-time traveler to Hua Hin or a returning visitor, these frequently asked questions address common queries and ensure a smooth and enjoyable experience. From practical information about currency and safety to cultural etiquette and culinary delights, being well-informed enhances your journey. It lets you maximize your time in this captivating coastal town.

Resources for a Seamless Hua Hin Adventure

Useful Websites and Apps

1. Tourism Authority of Thailand (TAT) – Hua Hin Office:

The official website of TAT provides comprehensive information about Hua Hin's attractions, events, and travel tips. Visit TAT Hua Hin for the latest updates and insights.

2. Google Maps:

Google Maps is an invaluable tool for navigating Hua Hin. Whether exploring the town, finding specific locations, or seeking directions, this app ensures you stay on the right track.

3. Grab:

Use the Grab app to book rides and estimate fares for hassle-free transportation. This service is convenient for securing reliable taxis or tuk-tuks with upfront pricing.

4. AccuWeather:

Stay informed about the weather conditions in Hua Hin with AccuWeather. This app provides accurate forecasts, helping you plan your outdoor activities accordingly.

5. XE Currency Converter:

The XE Currency Converter app is a handy resource for real-time currency conversions. Stay updated on exchange rates to manage your budget effectively during your stay.

Recommended Reading

1. "Hua Hin: Thailand's Royal Resort" by Carl Parkes:

This informative book delves into the history and charm of Hua Hin, offering insights into the town's development and its royal connections. It is a recommended read for those interested in understanding the cultural and historical aspects of Hua Hin.

2. "Lonely Planet Thailand" Guidebook:

The Lonely Planet guidebook for Thailand is a comprehensive resource that covers not only Hua Hin but the entire country. Packed with travel tips, cultural insights, and practical information, it's a valuable companion for any traveler exploring Thailand.

3. "Hua Hin – A Beach Resort Town in Thailand" by Andrew Forbes:

This guidebook by Andrew Forbes provides a detailed exploration of Hua Hin's attractions, activities, and cultural nuances. With vivid descriptions and practical tips, it's a useful companion for those planning to delve deep into the offerings of Hua Hin.

Emergency Contacts

1. Tourist Police – Hua Hin:

- **Contact Number:** 1155 (available 24/7)

- The Tourist Police in Hua Hin can assist travelers with various issues, including lost belongings, emergencies, and general inquiries. They are trained to handle situations involving tourists and provide guidance in multiple languages.

2. Hua Hin Hospital:

- **Contact Number:** +66 32 616 800

- In case of medical emergencies or health concerns, Hua Hin Hospital is a reputable medical facility with English-speaking staff. Keep this contact handy for any unforeseen circumstances.

3. Emergency Services – Police, Ambulance, Fire:

- **Emergency Number:** 191

- Dialing 191 connects you to emergency services in Hua Hin. Whether you need police assistance, medical help, or firefighting services, this universal emergency number is crucial for prompt response.

4. Embassy Contacts:

- **Your Country's Embassy or Consulate:** In case of more significant issues or emergencies, it's advisable to have the contact details of your country's embassy or consulate in Thailand. They can provide consular assistance and support.

5. Hua Hin Rescue:

- **Contact Number:** +66 32 511 111

- Hua Hin Rescue is a local organization that provides emergency medical services. Their trained personnel can respond quickly to accidents or health-related emergencies.

Before embarking on your Hua Hin journey, familiarize yourself with these resources to ensure a smooth and enjoyable experience. Whether you need real-time weather updates, reliable navigation tools, insightful reading material, or emergency contacts, these resources cater to various aspects of your trip. Stay informed, plan, and make the most of your time in this captivating coastal town.

Conclusion

As your Hua Hin adventure draws close, you've likely immersed yourself in the rich tapestry of experiences this coastal town offers. From the sun-kissed beaches to the vibrant markets, historical sites, and delectable cuisine, Hua Hin has woven a tapestry of memories that will linger long after you've bid farewell to its shores.

Reflecting on Cultural Immersion

Hua Hin's unique blend of modernity and tradition creates a captivating atmosphere for cultural exploration. Whether you've marveled at the intricate architecture of the Mrigadayavan Palace, engaged in the local art scene at Cicada Market, or embraced the warmth of the Thai people through cultural interactions, the town leaves an indelible mark on those seeking a deeper connection with the destination.

Unforgettable Culinary Journeys

The gastronomic delights of Hua Hin are a testament to the town's diverse culinary landscape. From savoring the bold flavors of local Thai delicacies to indulging in international cuisine at upscale restaurants, each meal is a journey through the vibrant palette of Hua Hin's culinary offerings. Whether you've explored the bustling Hua Hin Night Market or dined in a charming vintage village, the diverse culinary experiences add a flavorful dimension to your stay.

Outdoor Adventures and Relaxation

For the adventure-seekers, Hua Hin's outdoor activities provide an adrenaline rush against stunning landscapes. Whether you've engaged in water sports along the coast, teed off at world-class golf courses, or explored nature trails and viewpoints, Hua Hin caters to a spectrum of outdoor interests. Conversely, the serene beaches, spa retreats, and luxury resorts offer moments of relaxation, allowing you to unwind and rejuvenate in this coastal haven.

Navigating with Ease

Navigating the practical aspects of your journey in Hua Hin has been made seamless through the numerous resources available. From useful websites and apps guiding you through the town to recommended reading materials providing insights into its history and culture, these resources have enhanced your understanding and appreciation of Hua Hin. Understanding local transportation, cultural norms, and emergency contacts ensures a safe and well-informed exploration.

Cherished Souvenirs and Memories

As you pack your bags with souvenirs from vibrant markets and boutique stores, you carry tangible items and memories of an enriching cultural experience. Whether it's a piece of artwork from Cicada Market, a traditional Thai craft from a local artisan, or simply the scent of aromatic street food, these souvenirs serve as tangible reminders of the moments that have defined your Hua Hin journey.

Looking Ahead

Hua Hin leaves you with nostalgia and anticipation as you prepare to depart. The town's allure often beckons travelers to return, exploring new facets and uncovering hidden gems in subsequent visits. Whether you've reveled in the lively atmosphere of night markets, sought solace on pristine beaches, or immersed yourself in the vibrant arts and culture scene, Hua Hin remains etched in your travelogue as a destination that effortlessly blends tradition with modernity.

In conclusion, Hua Hin is more than a destination; it's an immersive experience that caters to diverse interests and preferences. It invites you to savor the flavors of Thai culture, embrace outdoor adventures, and unwind in its idyllic surroundings. As you bid farewell to Hua Hin, take with you the memories of the places you visited and the essence of a town that has seamlessly woven into your travel narrative. Until your next vacation, may the spirit of Hua Hin linger in your heart, a testament to the timeless charm of this coastal gem.

Made in United States
Orlando, FL
07 June 2024

47623645R00036